❂ SECRETS OF THE RAINFOREST ❂

PARTNERS AND PARENTS

BY MICHAEL CHINERY

❀ CRABTREE

Crabtree Publishing Company

PMB 16A, 350 Fifth Avenue Suite 3308
New York, NY
10118

612 Welland Avenue St. Catharines, Ontario
Canada L2M 5V6

Created by Cherrytree Press

© Evans Brothers Limited 2000

Library of Congress Cataloging-in-Publication Data

Chinery, Michael.
    Partners and parents / by Michael Chinery.
    p. cm.– (Secrets of the rainforest)
Summary: Describes some of the ways that various rainforest animals mate and raise their young.
    ISBN 0-7787-0216-2 (RLB) – ISBN 0-7787-0226-X (paper)
1. Rain forest animals–Behavior–Juvenile literature. 2.Courtship of animals–Juvenile literature.3. Parental behavior in animals–Juvenile literature [1. Rain forest animals–Habits and behavior. 2. Animals–Courtship. 3. Parental behavior in animals.] I. Title.
    QL112 .C53 2000
    591.734--dc21

LC 00-022067
CIP

Co-ordinating Editor: Ellen Rodger

Designed and produced by A S Publishing
Editor: Angela Sheehan
Design: Richard Rowan
Artwork: Malcolm Porter
Consultant: Sue Fogden

Acknowledgements
Photographs: *All by courtesy of Michael & Patricia Fogden with the following exceptions:*
BBC Natural History Unit
9 centre, 10, 26, 28, 29;
Michael Chinery
14 bottom, 15 bottom

1234567890
Prited in Hong Kong by
Wing King Tong. Ltd 543210

☀ CONTENTS ☀

❁ PARTNERS AND PARENTS ❁

RAINFORESTS grow in the **tropical** regions around the **equator**, where temperatures are high all year and where it rains nearly every day. Trees and other plants grow fast in these conditions. Animals also thrive in the warm climate and many make their homes, find mates, and bring up their young in the rainforests. There is danger in the rainforest as well. **Predators** are always ready to catch and eat other animals. Young animals are especially easy to prey upon.

With so many predators around, looking after the young is very important. Many rainforest animals are protected by **camouflage** or by being poisonous. Many others have developed ways that ensure their young are protected.

FENDING FOR THEMSELVES

Insects and many other small animals do not look after their young. Many insects and reptiles ensure the survival of their **offspring** by laying many eggs. Butterflies and moths lay eggs on leaves that will nourish the caterpillars hatching from them. Most of the caterpillars will be eaten by predators. Some will survive into adulthood just because there were so many eggs laid. Most frogs also lay large numbers of eggs, but do not care for the eggs after they are laid. The majority of these eggs or the **tadpoles** that hatch from them are eaten by predators. Only a few survive to become adult frogs.

▲ A pair of sunbitterns feed their chicks. Sunbitterns bring food to their nest and scare away intruders.

▼ A family group of tarsiers. Baby mammals drink their mother's milk and rely on their parents for their survival.

METAMORPHOSIS

MANY insects and other small animals lay eggs but do not care for their young. They do not live long themselves and cannot see the changes that their offspring go through. When a butterfly lays an egg, it hatches into a **larva** called a caterpillar. Caterpillars have stumpy legs and no wings. It eats and eats and eats, shedding its skin as it grows. After a while, the caterpillar becomes a **pupa**. As a pupa it does not move or eat, but its body slowly changes into that of an adult. The passionvine butterfly (left) has just emerged from its pupa, ready to begin its adult life. These changes are called **metamorphosis**, which means 'changing shape'. Frogs also metamorphose from eggs, to tadpoles, to frogs.

GOOD PARENTS

Animals that look after their eggs and young, such as birds and mammals, give them a much better chance of survival. They do not need to lay as many eggs or have many babies. Often after mating, males leave the females to raise the babies on their own. Some males help ensure the survival of their offspring. Male birds often catch most of the food for their young. Mammals often live in family groups. A baby mammal's survival depends on its access to its mother's milk. If a mammal mother dies or rejects its babies, the babies often do not survive.

▲ Most frogs lay many eggs, leave them and never see their offspring. The glass frog from the South American rainforest is different. The male and the female both guard their eggs.

▶ A mother eyelash viper and her brood. The newborn snakes are green or gold. Most snakes lay eggs but nearly all vipers give birth to live young.

❂ GUARDING A TERRITORY ❂

SOME ANIMALS have no permanent **territory**. They wander through the forest, alone or in groups, eating wherever they find food and sleeping wherever they happen to be when they are tired. Most animals have some kind of territory, which they defend against other animals of the same kind. The territory may belong to an individual or a family group. By establishing territories, animals ensure that they have plenty of room in which to find food.

South American howler monkeys warn other groups of howler monkeys to keep away from their territory by making a lot of noise. Many other animals mark the boundaries of the territories with strong scents. Fights sometimes break out on territory boundaries, but **intruders** usually go away as soon as the territory owner puts on a show of strength. A growl or the baring of teeth, or even puffing up feathers, may be enough to frighten an intruder away.

A territory is not always permanent. An animal or a group may defend an area of good food for just a few days or weeks, and then move on to establish a new one somewhere else.

HOME ON THE RANGE

Many animals, such as chimpanzees and gorillas, spend all of their lives roaming areas known as **home ranges**. The home ranges of large animals sometimes cover hundreds of square miles (or kilometers). The home ranges of small animals are only a few feet (or meters).

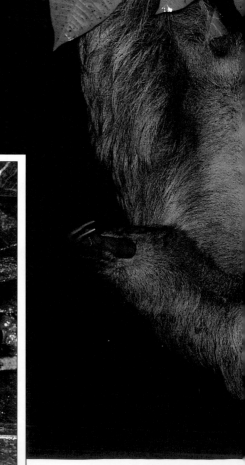

▼ These male strawberry arrow-poison frogs are fighting for a territory. The wrestling match may continue for hours until the weaker frog gives up.

► The umbrella bird has a fleshy wattle hanging from its chest which it inflates to attract a mate.

DISPLAY GROUNDS

D URING the **breeding** season the males of some birds and mammals gather in small areas and compete with each other to put on the best displays to attract females. These **communal** display grounds are not true territories and they are called leks. Several rainforest butterflies also gather in leks. The males release scent signals and the females choose the males with the strongest signals. The scents often come from the nectar that the butterflies collect from flowers. This glasswing butterfly is one of many rainforest species that attract females with scents.

Home ranges are not defended like territories. They often overlap those of other groups or families and neighboring groups of animals may meet and feed together, especially in areas with plenty of food.

BREEDING TERRITORIES

Territories are especially important when animals are protecting their young. This is generally the only time that animals make homes. Most birds build and occupy their nests only during the breeding season. The territory around the nest is defended by both male and female, and its size depends on the amount of food available. Large territories are needed if food is scarce.

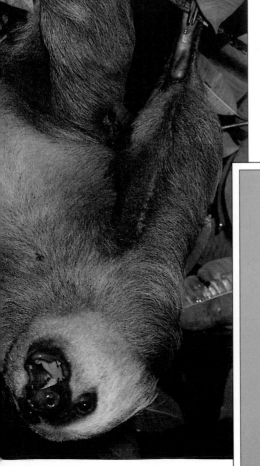

◄ Male sloths advertise their presence by smearing smelly *secretions* on to tree branches. Other males keep away, but females are attracted by the smell.

▼ The male three-wattled bellbird defends a large territory and attracts as many females to it as he can with his loud booming calls.

⟡ ATTRACTING A MATE ⟡

PRODUCING A NEW **generation** is very important for every **species**. For most animals, this means finding a **mate**. Like humans, many rainforest animals use color, scent, songs, and dances, and other **courtship behavior** to attract a mate. Female insects and mammals often attract males with a scent that tells them they are ready to mate. Male birds and bush-crickets attract females with songs. Many male birds also dance in front of the females and display their beautiful feathers.

Courtship songs and other displays bring males and females together. When animals mate, **sperm** passes from the males to the females and joins with the females' eggs. This is called **fertilization**. After fertilization, the eggs start to grow into new animals. Birds and many other animals lay their eggs soon after mating, but others, including most mammals, give birth to live young. The eggs develop inside, rather than outside, the females' bodies.

▲ During their courtship dance, the male scorpion drops a package of sperm and guides the female over it. She scoops it up and later gives birth to many babies.

▼ These giant millipedes from South America coil around each other to mate. The female will lay many eggs in the soil and then leave.

▼ A male tree frog sings to attract a female. The balloon-like pouch under his neck vibrates and magnifies the sound. Each kind of frog has its own call so that it attracts only females of its own species.

▲ A wire-tailed manakin and his helper jump up and down to attract a female. As soon as a female arrives, the younger bird is sent on his way.

▶ A male cock-of-the-rock will join other birds in a group *courtship* display. If a female is interested she will peck him on his hind.

WHAT A PERFORMANCE!

Male birds of paradise perform dazzling courtship displays to attract females. The males swing on the branches of trees or dance on the ground, displaying their long, colorful **plumes** in all directions. Each bird performs alone for one female and they soon become mates.

The male cock-of-the-rock has brilliant orange **plumage**, like a flame on the rainforest floor. Rather than each male courting a particular female, the males put on a communal display that is something between a dance and a gymnastic routine. The females watch as the males strut and then each one indicates her choice of partner by pecking him from behind.

Manakin bird males use one or more younger birds to assist with their courtship display. The birds jump up and down on a branch as if bouncing on a trampoline. As one comes down, another goes up, singing all the while. When a female starts to show interest in the performance, the **dominant** bird whistles sharply and the assistants fly away, leaving the dominant bird to mate with the female.

COME INTO MY GARDEN

Bower birds are not particularly colorful, but they have a colorful courtship practice. To attract a mate, the male makes a love-nest. He builds a **bower** of twigs and then decorates it with flowers, berries, colorful shells, and even bits of colored paper and glass. The females select the males with the best bowers. Some male bower birds seem to get jealous and steal the brightest objects from other males. Sometimes they even destroy another male's bower. After mating in the bowers, the females go off to build their nests and raise their families alone.

LIGHTING THE FOREST

Fireflies are a type of beetle. They signal to their mates with flashes of light that look like flashlights going on and off. Each species has its own pattern of flashing, with its own time interval between the flashes. Their sense of timing is so accurate that they can recognize the flashes of their own species and ignore those of other species. Fireflies live in many parts of the world, but the most spectacular live in Southeast Asia. Thousands of males gather in **mangrove** trees and flash together like a neon sign. The females fly to the trees and mate with the males.

▲ A Wilson's bird of paradise attracts a female with his beautiful plumage. Birds of paradise all live on the island of New Guinea and neighboring areas of Indonesia and on the northern tip of Australia.

ONE PARTNER OR MANY

IN THIS writhing ball of snakes (left) as many as ten male anacondas are attempting to mate with one female. In many species there is often intense **competition** for mates. One female may be courted by many males, and the males often fight each other. The female mates with the winner and, because he is strong, he will probably father healthy offspring. Most animals split up after mating and may never see each other again, although some males stay around long enough to help with the babies. A few animals stay together for life once they have mated, but most species have several or many partners during their lives.

▼ A female bower bird has accepted the male's invitation into his bower. After mating, the female will build a nest for her eggs and young.

BREEDING ALL YEAR

IN MOST parts of the world animals have mating seasons. Birds, for example, usually mate in spring. Many tropical forests, especially those in the lowlands, remain warm and moist throughout the year, and plants never stop growing. Animals, like these delicate handkerchief butterflies performing their courtship dance, can breed at any time of the year. Many insects grow up in just three or four weeks and produce several generations in a year.

⚙ INSECTS THAT LIVE TOGETHER ⚙

ANTS AND termites have the largest families of all rainforest animals. They are **social insects** that live in huge family groups called colonies. The individuals all work for the good of the community as a whole.

ZILLION-MEMBER FAMILIES

Walk anywhere in the South American rainforest at night and you are likely to see columns of ants marching along, waving bits of leaves above their heads, and then disappearing underground. These are leaf-cutter ants. Their nests are huge. They are sometimes as big as a bus. The ants dig the soil out themselves and pile it outside the nest. The heap of soil outside one nest in Brazil weighed 44 tons (40 tonnes). A queen and up to eight million worker ants live in the nest, which may have over a thousand little rooms or chambers. The queen is the mother of all the ants in the nest. The workers are her daughters.

▲ Leaf-cutter ants can travel over 328 feet (100 meters) to collect leaves, which they cut into sections. They remove every leaf from a plant before attacking the next one.

PLANT PARTNERS

A NTS not only work with each other, some also enter into partnerships with the plants they live on. Many tropical plants, including the climbing palms or rattans and some of the acacia trees, are home to fierce ants. The ants swarm out and sting any animal that starts to nibble the plant's leaves. The plants are protected by their guests. Some of the plants provide food for the ants in the form of honey-like nectar. This meat-eating ant (right) is protecting a passion flower.

Many epiphytic plants have swollen bases that have many small chambers where various ants live. The ants protect the plants from attack and their droppings also provide the plants with valuable food.

▼ Leaf-cutter ants are also called parasol ants because they hold the cut leaves like sunshades. Their nests (left) may be 6.5 feet (two metres) or more deep and wide.

FAMILY FARMS

To feed a colony, leaf-cutter ants have developed a remarkable skill. They have become farmers by growing tiny mushrooms in special gardens. Every day at sunset, many thousands of the ants stream from their nests and head for the trees. They use their scissor-like jaws to carve pieces from the leaves, and then carry the pieces back to their nests. They give the leaf fragments to smaller workers. These smaller ants chew the leaf fragments into a soggy pulp, which they put into one of many special garden chambers. They add some of the **fungus** from an existing garden and often add their own droppings as a manure-like **fertilizer.** The fungus grows rapidly on the pulped leaves and soon covers them with fluffy threads. Little swellings form at the tips of the threads and the workers gather them for food. Old fungus gardens are regularly thrown on to the heap of soil around the nest.

TEEMING TERMITES

There are hundreds of different kinds of termites. They are like ants, but not related to them. Termites are all **vegetarians**, feeding on seeds, leaves and dead wood. Some termites grow fungi on dead leaves just like leaf-cutter ants. Termites do terrible damage to buildings in rainforest areas and in other parts of the tropics.

Many termite species live under the ground or hidden in dead wood. Some make small nests on the branches of rainforest trees, others build huge mounds of earth. Some of them stick soil particles together with **saliva** to make roads from their nests to their feeding grounds. Some termites even build roofs over their roads so that they can reach their feeding grounds without exposing themselves to light or to their many predators. Their pale, soft bodies are very tasty and many birds and other animals like to eat them.

KING AND QUEEN

A large termite colony contains millions of insects and is ruled by a single queen who does nothing but lay eggs. Her sausage-like body pumps out as many as 30,000 eggs every day.

▲ A termite nest that has been damaged. Soldiers swarm over the exposed surface to attack a predator, while the other termites scurry away to safety.

▼ A group of termite soldiers can quickly stop an attacker by firing streams of sticky fluid from their tubular snouts.

AIR-CONDITIONED HOMES

BIG termite nests contain hundreds of rooms in which the insects store their food and raise their young. The rooms are linked by hundreds of narrow passages. Some of the biggest nests even have air-conditioning systems to stop them from getting too hot. Each kind of termite has developed its own system. In one system, chimney-like tubes allow the hot, stale air to escape. Fresh air flows in through holes near the bottom and keeps the whole nest fresh and cool.

Termites living in rainforests often build mushroom-shaped nests or they add umbrella-shaped roofs (right) to keep the rain out.

The other termites work hard to feed and clean the queen. The queen lives with a king, who is much smaller than she is. The other termites in the colony are all the children of the king and queen. Most of them are workers and, although they are blind, they collect all the food and do all the building work. There are also some soldier termites, with big heads and jaws, whose job is to defend the colony. They bite anything that tries to break into the nest, although anteaters and some other animals are not stopped by their bites.

The termites in a colony are always licking each other and exchanging food. This helps to spread **pheromones**, the chemical messengers that ensure that they all behave properly and do the right things at the right times. Many of the pheromones come from the queen.

From time to time, the termite colony raises new kings and queens, and these fly out from the nest in huge swarms. Birds and other animals feast for hours on these swarms. The few termites that avoid the predators and get back to earth break off their wings and pair up to start new colonies.

☀ FROG FAMILIES ☀

FROGS cannot live far from water because they have thin skins. Without water, frogs would shrivel and die in dry air. They also have to lay their eggs in water. In most places they live near ponds, but in the rainforests it is so damp that they can make their homes in the trees. The forests are also full of insects so the frogs are never short of food.

Hundreds of different kinds of frogs live in rainforests. Many spend all their lives in the trees and do not even come down to **breed**. They are active in the evening and at night, when there are fewer predators around to eat them. To attract females, the males sing loudly and the night air is full of their assorted clicks, squeaks and whistles, some of which are very musical. When in full song, the forest frogs drown out nearly all the other sounds.

▶ Mosquito larvae living in rainwater pools provide food for baby frogs.

▲ A male glass frog, transparent and almost invisible on a leaf, sits close to its jelly-like masses of eggs to protect them. It will also bring water to the eggs to prevent the eggs from drying up.

◄ This flying frog glides down from the tree-tops to mate and lay its eggs on leaves that are overhanging water. The tadpoles fall into the water when they hatch.

► The colorful underside of this barred leaf frog helps it attract a mate and break up its outline as it moves. Tree frogs do not normally hop like most other frogs, they crawl slowly on their long slender legs.

TREE-TOP NURSERIES

The branches of rainforest trees are covered with various small plants called **epiphytes**. Many of these plants collect rainwater in their crowns of spiky leaves. Some tree frogs lay their eggs in the little pools created by the leaves. Mosquito larvae and lots of other small creatures also live in the pools and provide food for the tadpoles that hatch from the eggs. Hidden among the spiky leaves, the tadpoles are also protected from many of their enemies.

WRESTLING MALES

Strawberry **arrow-poison frogs** are as brightly colored and poisonous as their name suggests. Males adopt territories on the ground, each one choosing an area with plenty of water plants, such as **bromeliads**, that will provide homes for the tadpoles. The male guards his territory and tries hard to attract females by calling to them continuously. Other males that enter the area are forced out. Neighboring males often fight, clutching each other like wrestlers and rolling over and over on the forest floor. They shove and kick each other until both are exhausted.

BABY-SITTER

Once a female strawberry arrow-poison frog has accepted a male and mated, she lays her eggs under a dead leaf. Unlike many other amphibians, the female strawberry arrow-poison frog only lays about ten eggs. The male sits by the eggs for a couple of weeks and then the tadpoles emerge and crawl on to the female's back. She carries them to the bromeliad plants and drops them into the little pools. There is plenty of water for them to swim in, but not a lot food, so she drops just one tadpole into each plant. The female later adds to the food supply by laying extra eggs in the plants. The tadpoles use these eggs for food.

POND BUILDERS

One Brazilian tree frog builds its own private pool in shallow water at the edge of a pond or stream. The male collects mud with his front feet and, using the broad pads on the tips of

FROG IN A POUCH

$\mathbf{M}$ARSUPIAL frogs carry their offspring around with them. The female of this pygmy marsupial frog from Venezuela (above) has a large pouch on her back and, after fertilizing the eggs, the male guides them into the pouch.

▼ One by one, a mother strawberry arrow-poison frog carries her tadpoles on her back to its own private pool in a bromeliad.

▲ Safe in its pool, a baby arrow-poison frog waits for its mother. She will check that there is enough water in the pool and lay more eggs for it to eat.

The eggs hatch in the pouch and the tadpoles live there for a while, nourished by food stored in the eggs. Even when they turn into froglets, the young of some species continue to be carried by their parents. They are not released into the water until they are very big.

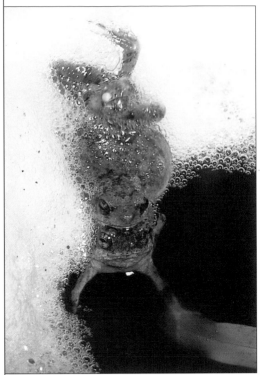

NESTS OF BUBBLES

SEVERAL kinds of frogs, including these Central American tungara frogs, protect their eggs by covering them with foam. The female produces a lot of slime with her eggs, and then the male and female whip it into a foam with their feet. The outer layer of foam may dry and form a hard skin, keeping the inner layers moist, but the females of some species keep the whole nest moist by periodically collecting water and spraying it over the foam. These foam nests are formed on leaves overhanging a pool or stream. When the eggs hatch, the foam turns to liquid and the tadpoles fall into the water below.

▼ A Darwin's frog male with two of his offspring. Until they are big enough to fend for themselves, the adult frog keeps them in his throat pouch.

his fingers, moulds it into a circular wall about 12 inches (30 cm) across. When complete, the wall stands about 4 inches (10 cm) above the surrounding water. The frog then starts his love song with a loud, droning call that sounds like a hammer on steel. This attracts the female, who lays her eggs in the pool, where they are safe from enemies. The tadpoles stay inside the wall for a while, but eventually it crumbles and they escape into the surrounding water.

· FORESTS FULL OF NESTS ·

THERE IS a lot of nest-building material in the rainforests. Rainforest birds build many different kinds of nests. They sew, weave, and stick plant materials together to make homes for their eggs and nestlings.

WEAVER ANTS

Weaver ants are not well named. The ants do not weave but make their nests by sticking leaves together with a natural glue. The ants pull several leaves together to form a bag or pouch by gripping the edges with their hind feet and their powerful jaws.

▼ Green weaver ants live in the tropical forests of Africa, Asia, and Australia. Each colony defends its territory against ants from other nests.

▶ This leaf-rolling spider from Borneo guards its eggs and young inside a rolled leaf. The female also shelters there while waiting for prey to arrive.

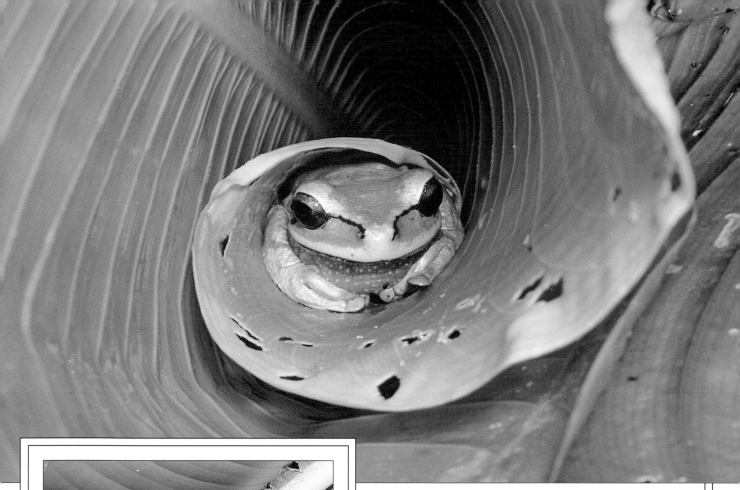

▲ Masked puddle frogs make temporary homes in the curled young leaves of heliconia plants. There, they stay moist and hidden from their predators during the daytime.

If the gap is too wide for one ant to stretch across it, two or more link their legs to form chains, and then they all pull together to bring the edges of the leaves into line.

Ants carrying young grubs start to run in a zigzag fashion along the joins. The grubs give out strands of sticky silk, which the adult ants fix to each side of the join. The silk soon hardens and the leaves are held firmly together. A mature nest may be nearly as big as a football but, because the leaves are still attached to the tree and remain green, the nests are not easy to see. Any animal that does find a nest is in for a shock. Weaver ants protect their nests by biting viciously.

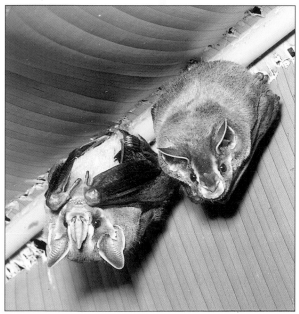

TREE-TOP TENTS

S EVERAL kinds of bats make neat little shelters for themselves by nibbling through the veins of leaves so that the leaf blades flop down like tent roofs. The tents keep the bats perfectly dry, despite the forest's heavy rainfall, and also conceal them from predators. Some of the bats even have their babies in the tents and leave them there while they go out to feed.

WEAVING BIRDS

The male oropendola bird courts the female with a noisy dance, during which he raises his tail and wings and bows so low that he almost topples from his perch. The birds nest in colonies and build dozens of nests in a single tree. The nests are built by the females, while their mates keep watch and sing from nearby perches. Each nest is like a large sock, up to a 3 feet (one meter) long and woven from strips of palm leaves. Each one hangs from the swaying tip of a branch, where few predators can reach it. Several kinds of oropendolas live in the rainforests of Central and South America, each one building to a slightly different design.

The weaver birds of Africa build similar nests, but there it is the male who starts the building work.

▼ Part of a colony of chestnut-headed oropendolas in Central America. Strong winds can damage the nests, so the birds usually build them in sheltered spots.

TREE-TOP CRADLES
. . . .

HUMMINGBIRDS are the smallest of all birds. Twigs and most other plant materials are too big and coarse to make good nesting material for these tiny birds. Instead, they gather plant hairs and silk from spiders' webs to build little cup-shaped nests. Some include soft petals as well to make a satiny lining for their nestlings' cradle.

◀ The straight-billed hermit, a kind of hummingbird, builds its nest with plant hairs and spider silk and fixes it at the tip of a large, drooping leaf.

▲ These two blue-throated goldentail hummingbird chicks are about to leave their tiny nest, made from spider silk. It has been their home for three weeks.

▼ The nest of the white-throated spadebill, made from tightly-woven plant fibers, is attached to a slender twig.

When he is about half way through he tries to interest a female in his work, and if she likes what she sees, she moves in and finishes the job. Most weaver birds live in open country, but the village weaver likes to build on the edges of forest villages. Its ball-shaped nests hang from the tips of the branches and palm leaves, and weigh them down like large fruits.

A TAILORED NEST

The tailor bird deserves its name, because it really does sew its nest together. It chooses a large leaf or sometimes two smaller ones and sews the edges together to form a bag. Its sharp, pointed beak makes a good needle. Thread is made from cottony fibers stripped from plants and spun into longer strands, or from bark fibers or even silk strands from spiders' webs. As the tailor bird sews, it ties knots in the thread to keep it in place. When it is finished, the bird lines the nest with soft fibers. Because the nest is made from living leaves still attached to the tree, it is hard to find it in the dense forest. Tailor birds live in southern Asia. When living close to villages, they often sew their nests with bits of string and cotton discarded by the villagers.

WALLED UP

Hornbills have huge beaks that they use for stretching out to reach fruit at the tips of slender branches. Their bills are long but very light and not powerful. Their bills are not good for digging a nest hole. When a female hornbill is ready to nest, she has to find an existing hole in a tree that suits her needs. She settles inside and for up to three months afterwards remains a prisoner in the hole. Her mate brings her mud and she uses it like cement to block up the entrance hole until only a narrow slit remains. The slit is just big enough for her to poke her beak out to take food from the male. Inside her prison, she lays her eggs and rears her **nestlings**. When the chicks are two or three weeks old, the mother bird breaks out of her prison, but the young birds immediately seal up the hole again to keep themselves safe from predators. The male and female both continue to bring food for the growing nestlings. Only when they are strong enough to fly do the little birds come out of prison.

▲ A male knobbed hornbill from Indonesia perches by its nest hole, which the female has started to wall up with mud.

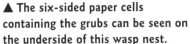

◀ A male resplendent quetzal feeds its hungry chick with its favorite food – a nutritious wild avocado.

▲ The six-sided paper cells containing the grubs can be seen on the underside of this wasp nest.

◀ The slaty-backed nightingale-thrush from Central America builds a bulky nest with mosses and other plants and fixes it firmly in a bush.

PAPER NESTS

Many species of wasps live in the rainforests and some build remarkable nests of paper – the chewed fibers of plants. The nest is started by the queen after she has mated. She chews up the paper and spreads it out in layers that she forms into little cells where she lays her eggs. The eggs hatch and eventually turn into small female worker wasps. They go to work immediately, building new cells for new eggs. The eggs turn into larvae and the workers feed them with food they have collected. This is usually the flesh of insects and other small animals that the wasps have caught and torn to pieces with their tough jaws. They chew the flesh and swallow it, and bring it up again to feed the grubs in the nest. These grubs grow into more workers, which build more cells for more eggs: the nest grows and grows.

◀ This male golden-browed chlorophonia from Central America has collected material for its cup-shaped nest that will hold up to five nestlings. It belongs to a group of brightly-colored birds called tanagers.

· MONKEYS AND APES ·

MOST RAINFOREST mammals are solitary animals that raise their young alone. Monkeys and apes often form large family **clans** that fiercely guard a territory. Not all monkeys form clans. Some live in small family groups, with just a male and female and their youngsters. Others form **harems**, in which one male lives with several females and their offspring.

Monkeys and apes do not make permanent homes, even when raising their babies. They wander freely over their territories or home ranges and sleep wherever they happen to be when it gets dark.

▶ The vivid colors on the male mandrill's face warn intruders to keep away and younger members of the group to keep their place. They also attract females to mate with him.

TROOPS OF MONKEYS

Howler monkeys live in clans, or troops, each containing several adult males and females and young monkeys of all ages. There may be 30 or more monkeys in a clan and they 'talk' to each other with a wide variety of sounds. Clicking sounds help to keep the clan together when scampering through the tree-tops. Loud howls warn of approaching danger, but the loudest sounds are reserved for territorial defense. When they wake in the morning, the animals set up a deafening chorus of howls and roars that can be heard as much as 2 miles (5 km) away. The howling warns other clans of howler monkeys to keep away for the rest of the day.

◀ A crab-eating macaque from Bali sits on the remains of an ancient temple and tends its baby. Babies are shared by all the monkeys in a troop. They are often passed around for other females to cuddle.

▼ A crested black macaque keeps watch for any dangers as it sits on the ground with its baby.

◀ Not all monkeys form large clans. Some, like these golden-lion tamarins, live in small groups of just a male and female with their offspring.

CHIMPANZEE CLANS

Chimpanzees are apes and the nearest living relatives of human beings. They live in Africa in loosely organized clans that can contain 100 or more. Small groups of chimpanzees often break away and wander off on their own for a while. A clan has no assigned leader. Adult males sometimes boss the other clan members but all the clan members usually get along well with each other.

Chimpanzees are at home on the ground and in the trees. They usually sleep high in the trees, where they are safe from leopards. They make new beds nearly every night by twisting leafy branches together. Even when they have young babies, chimpanzees do not make nests.

Baby chimpanzees are carried around by their mothers as soon as they are born. There are always babies in the clan and the females all help to look after them. The young chimpanzees stay close to their mothers for five or six years, and spend a lot of this time playing with other youngsters. The males take little interest in the babies.

▶ A silverback gorilla is respected and obeyed by the whole troop. He may be challenged occasionally, by younger males hoping to win his females.

▼ A young chimpanzee begs an older member of the clan for a share of its meat. Watching how the adults collect fruit and catch and kill food is an important part of a young chimp's training.

▲ Orangutans are large apes of Southeast Asia. Adults live alone, although babies stay with their mothers for three years.

GROOMING

MONKEYS and apes spend many hours contentedly grooming each other. One animal combs and searches the fur of another. They lick and run their fingers through each other's fur. When an animal wants to be groomed, it usually approaches another and offers an arm or some other part of its body. As well as removing lice and other parasites and keeping the fur clean, grooming is a social activity. It helps to calm the animals and it brings members of the clan together. Animals that have spent time grooming each other are likely to help each other in times of trouble.

GORILLAS

The gorilla is the largest of the apes. A big male, standing nearly 6.5 feet (2 meters) high and weighing nearly 440 pounds (200 kg), can look fierce. Gorillas are really very peaceful. Gorillas live in the rainforests of West and Central Africa. They are too heavy to do a lot of climbing, so they live mainly on the ground. At night they sleep on beds or cushions made from leafy branches. These are usually just above the ground, although small gorillas may make their beds in the trees.

Gorillas live in small clans. There are between 10 and 15 animals in a clan, and it is ruled by an old male. He has silvery grey hair on his back and is called a silverback. The clan also contains several females and younger gorillas of various ages, and there may be one or more blackback males. Blackbacks are fully grown gorillas, without the silvery grey hair. Every animal knows its place in the clan and there is hardly ever any fighting. Junior members always move aside for older ones. The silverback makes all the decisions, such as when to get up in the morning, which way to wander, and when to eat. Young gorillas stay with their mothers for six years, during which time they learn the meaning of the sounds and signs used by clan members. They soon learn who is the boss of the clan.

▼ A young gorilla explores his surroundings. Gorillas have few enemies. The biggest threat to their survival is from the destruction of their forest *habitat* by humans.

❊ GLOSSARY ❊

Arrow-poison frog Any of a number of South American frogs whose poison is used on darts and arrows. Also called poison-dart frogs.

Bower A shaded leafy arbor

Breed To breed is to reproduce, or have babies.

Bromeliad Any of a number of plants, related to pineapples, with crowns of stiff leaves. The crowns hold pools of water. Many bromeliads grow as epiphytes on the branches of trees.

Camouflage Colors and patterns that help an animal blend with its surroundings and avoid its predators.

Canopy The 'roof' of the rainforest, formed by the leafy branches of the trees. It is usually about 98 feet (30 meters) above the ground and it cuts off most of the light from the forest floor.

Clan The name given to a group of monkeys or apes that live together like a big family.

Communal Living together as part of an organized community.

Courtship The behavior of males and females that brings them together for mating and reproduction.

Dominant The dominant animal in a community is the leader – the individual that controls the others.

Epiphyte Any plant that grows on another, especially on the branches of a tree, but takes no food from it. Ferns, orchids, and bromeliads are common epiphytes in the rainforests.

Equator An imaginary line around the center of the earth, midway between the north and south poles.

Fertilization The joining of a sperm from a male animal with an egg from a female.

Fungi (singular fungus) Plant-like organisms that grow without sunlight and take their food from living or dead plants and animals. Mushrooms and molds are all fungi.

Generation Offspring that descend from a common ancestor. Parents and children belong to different generations but the same ancestors.

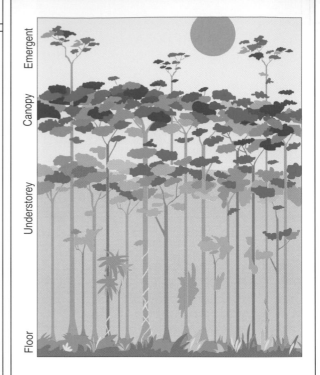

▲ A rainforest has layers of vegetation: fungi and low-growing plants on the forest floor, slender, young, branchless trees that form an understorey below the vast, dense *canopy* of tree-tops. Taller trees called emergents, sometimes poke their heads through the canopy.

Habitat The natural home of a plant or animal species. It may be a whole forest or just a tree trunk, or even a pool of water trapped by a plant.

Harem A group of adult females living with, and controlled by, a single male. The male mates with all the females in the group.

Home range An area inhabited by an animal or a group of animals but not defended against other animals of the same kind.

Intruder Someone who enters a territory without permission or invitation.

Larva (plural larvae) Stage in the development of some animals. Caterpillars and tadpoles are larvae.

Mangrove An evergreen tree whose stilt-like roots form dense tangles in coastal swamps.

Mate Animals mate with each other to produce offspring. The male passes sperm from his body to combine with the eggs of the female. Each is the other's mate.

Metamorphosis The changes in shape of some animals that take place as they grow up.

ENDANGERED!

R AINFORESTS are home to more plants and animals that any other habitat on earth. They are important to the world but they are in danger of destruction. Many of the animals and plants shown in this book are endangered. Their rainforest habitat is slowly being destroyed by humans. If you are interested in knowing more about rainforests and in helping to conserve them, you may find these addresses and websites useful.

Friends of the Earth
USA - 1025 Vermont Ave NW, 3rd floor,
Washington, DC, 20005-6303
Canada - 47 Clarence St. Suite 306,
Ottawa, ON, K1N 9K1

Rainforest Foundation, U.S.
270 Lafayette Street, Suite 1107
New York, NY, 10012 USA

Rainforest Alliance
65 Bleecker Street, New
York, NY,
10012 USA

Rainforest Action Network
221 Pine Street, Suite 500
San Francisco, CA
94104 USA

Greenpeace
USA- 1436 U Street NW
Washington, DC, 20009, USA
Canada - 250 Dundas Street West, Suite 605
Toronto, ON, M5T 2Z5, Canada

Rainforest Alliance
http://www.rainforest-alliance.org

Friends of the Earth
http://www.foecanada.org
http://www.foe.org/FOE

Environmental Education Network
http://envirolink.org.enviroed/

Greenpeace
http://greenpeace.org

◀ **The map shows the location of the world's main rainforest areas.**

Nestling A young bird that has not yet left its nest.

Pheromone A chemical signal or scent given out by one animal and causing another animal of the same kind to behave in a particular way. Pheromones help to keep ant colonies working properly, and they also bring male and female animals together for mating.

Plumage The feathers of a bird. A plume is any particularly large or attractive feather.

Predator Any animal that hunts and kills other animals for food.

Primate Any member of the order of mammals containing the monkeys and apes. Human beings are primates, and so are tarsiers and bushbabies.

Pupa The stage in an insect's life during which it changes from a larva or caterpillar into an adult.

Saliva A fluid secreted by glands in or around the mouth. It lubricates food and often helps to

digest it. Many insects mix saliva with mud and other materials and use the mixture for building their nests.

Social insects Insects that live in communities and work together for the good of the whole group. They include termites and ants and some bees and wasps.

Sperm A male cell that can join with a female egg cell to produce a new cell from which a new animal can grow.

Tadpole Name given to the young stages of frogs and toads.

Territory An area inhabited by an animal or a group of animals, and defended against other animals of the same kind.

Tropical Describes the tropics — the warm areas around the equator.

Vegetarian Any animal that feeds mainly on plants.

❋ INDEX ❋